Franklin Harvey Head

Studies in early American history

The legends of Jekyl Island

Franklin Harvey Head

Studies in early American history
The legends of Jekyl Island

ISBN/EAN: 9783741190544

Manufactured in Europe, USA, Canada, Australia, Japa

Cover: Foto ©ninafisch / pixelio.de

Manufactured and distributed by brebook publishing software
(www.brebook.com)

Franklin Harvey Head

Studies in early American history

STUDIES

IN

EARLY AMERICAN HISTORY

THE

Legends of Jekyl Island

BY

FRANKLIN H. HEAD

Magna est veritas, et prevalebit.

Truth, crushed to earth, shall rise again,
The eternal years of God are hers,
But Error, wounded, writhes with pain,
And dies amid her worshippers.

CHICAGO
PRIVATELY PRINTED

Studies in

Early American History.

THE LEGENDS OF

JEKYL ISLAND.

.. .. .. BY .. .. ..

FRANKLIN H. HEAD.

THE LEGENDS OF JEKYL ISLAND

GEN. JAMES E. OGLETHORPE.

By permission, from the original painting by Sir Joshua Reynolds, now owned by Mr. Clarence King, of New York.

TO MY VALUED FRIEND,

EDWARD G. MASON,

PRESIDENT OF THE CHICAGO HISTORICAL SOCIETY,

AND AUTHOR OF

"THE HISTORY OF ILLINOIS,"

NOT ALONE AS A MARK OF HIGH PERSONAL ESTEEM, BUT
IN RECOGNITION OF HIS EQUALLY PAINSTAKING AND
ACCURATE LABORS IN SIMILAR FIELDS
OF HISTORICAL RESEARCH.

The Legends of Jekyl Island.

SOME years since, during the same week, I heard Jekyl Island described from two standpoints. It was soon after its purchase by an association of gentlemen forming the well-known Jekyl Island Club. Two of my friends gave me a glowing account of this newly found island of Atlantis. A semi-tropical island off the coast of southern Georgia; 17,000 acres of beautiful land, mostly covered with choice timber, 1,400 deer ranging the forest, green turtle marching in uninterrupted procession along the silvery beach, a lake of 500 acres so packed with terrapin as to resemble a cedar block pavement, flocks of quail and partridge darkening the air, oysters of incomparable flavor everywhere, and all purchased at an unheard of bargain, for the beggarly pittance of $125,000.

Once in every man's life comes to him his opportunity, and my two friends felt and rejoiced that theirs had nor passed unheeded by, for each had secured a share in this enchanted island.

A few days later I met and chatted with a man whom many of us in Chicago remember as Jim Kelly, who was on a visit to Chicago from his Florida plantation. Said Jim, " I like Florida just because I'm well there and am not well anywhere else. A man with an orange grove can get a modest living, but when it comes to doing business or making money, of course the chances in any part of the South are comparatively small. Still," continued Jim, "sometimes a man gets struck by lightning even there. I have a cousin who owned an island off the Georgia coast, 17,000 acres of sand and swamp. You couldn't raise anything on it; there was some scattering, but utterly worthless, timber. He had tried for years to sell it, to trade it off, or to mortgage it, but he couldn't do either. In fact," concluded Jim, "the whole thing wasn't worth a damn, but lately he picked up a lot of rich suckers from New York, Boston and Chicago, and sold them his Jekyl Island for $125,000."

I recognized with interest and delight, as
often before, the widely variant conclusions
from the points of view; and when, in the
spring of 1892, my friends King and McCagg,
who were members of the club, invited me to
visit the island as their guest, I accepted with
delight, eager to see for myself the picture
which had been before me in such contrasted
lights.

I found the March climate of the island in-
vigorating and delightful; the bridle paths and
roads through the forest wisely planned and
charming; the drive of a dozen miles along the
firm and shining beach the joy of a lifetime.
The absence of the 1,400 deer, the quail, part-
ridges and terrapin was explained by the
statement that the committee of three who
visited the island prior to its purchase, had
eaten them, although a tradition is still current
that on a certain remote and possibly mythical
Sunday, terrapin soup was served to some of
the early inhabitants.

The club house was well planned for its pur-
pose; the company choice, intellectual and in

every way agreeable. All members of the club worthy of their exalted heritage were busily employed in doing nothing and in doing it thoroughly and well. A few members who were looking about for something to do, who watched anxiously for the newspapers and sought to adulterate the atmosphere of the island, with the airs and cares of the outer world, were frowned upon, and their expulsion would have been considered, except that the consideration of even so self-evident a necessity would have required an effort. The Vice President and acting executive, of dignified and stately presence, was a man of abounding energy and fire, which was exercised daily and hourly in the transferring until the day after to-morrow of the things which should have been done yesterday. In a word, the island is an ideal resting place for the man of affairs. The visitors during my stay were largely of middle life, upon whom ease with dignity sat gracefully. Yet even there, and among them, the sprightly arrow-shooting god played havoc, and one of the loved and honored members, in sequence thereof, met there smilingly his doom, and now wanders, no longer alone, in far away Cathay, hand in hand with his happy fate, and renews under occidental skies the dreams of his golden youth.

I found upon the island certain ruins, pre-historic, so far as the present inhabitants were informed, but concerning which sundry and contradictory legends were current. The general trend of the local folklore was that the island had once belonged to General Ogle-thorpe, the founder and governor of the Georgia colony. A solitary chimney was supposed to mark the site of the gubernatorial palace. Certain mounds and pits near the shore were, by the different schools of archæologists upon the island, variously claimed to represent the work of the Aztec Mound Builders, diggings for the buried treasures of Captain Kidd, and earth-works erected during the late war to protect blockade runners escaping to the Bermudas. In view of these conflicting theories, and of the lack of accurate information on the part even of the members of the Jekyl Island Club,

the antiquarian zeal, the frenzy, a la Herodo-
tus, which, radiating from the President of the
Chicago Historical Society, animates all its
members, urged me to learn what I could of the
history of the island, and I place before my
readers the results of much painstaking research
in this field.

The first mention I have been able to find of
Jekyl Island occurs in a report made to Queen
Elizabeth in 1587, by Sir Francis Drake. This
gallant admiral had captured and mercilessly
plundered the Spanish towns of Saint Jago,
Cartagena and Saint Augustine, and after leaving the last named point, sailed northerly along
the coast for some hundreds of miles. His
report to Queen Elizabeth runs thus:

"On the 17th we took an observation, and
found ourselves in latitude 30 deg. 30 min. N.,
and near a large island, which we felt sure was
the land where we had information of a Spanish
settlement of magnitude. Seeing some log
houses, we decided to make a landing. We
unfurled the standard of Saint George and
approached the shore in great force, that we

SIR FRANCIS DRAKE.

From the portrait by Titian now in the gallery of the Marquis of Queensberry.

might impress the enemy with the great puissance of your Majesty. The accursed Spaniards, concealed behind the trees, fired upon us, and a sore and cruel fight seemed pendent, when the enemy, stricken with fear, incontinently fled to their homes, with their habiliments of war. One of our men was sorely wounded by the Spanish Captain, whom we presently made prisoner, and, having set up a gallows, we there hanged him in a chain by the middle, and afterwards consumed with fire, gallows and all.

To us was the good God most merciful and gracious, in that he permitted us to kill eighteen Spaniards, bitter enemies of your sweet Majesty. We further wasted the country and brought it to utter ruin. We burned their houses and killed their few horses, mules and cattle, eating what we could of the fresh beef and carrying the rest aboard our ships. Having in mind the merciful disposition of your gracious Majesty, we did not kill the women and children, but having destroyed upon the island all their provisions and property, and taken away all their weapons, we left them to starve.

In view was another considerable island, fifteen miles to the northward, concerning which we asked of the women if any Spaniards dwelt thereon. The women were most ungracious, sullen and obstinate, perchance from their husbands having been killed before their eyes, and wickedly refused to answer us, but after we had burned a hole with a hot iron through the tongue of the most venomous of their number, they eftsoons told us that there were no Spaniards upon the other island; that it was the haunt of a solitary Frenchman named Jacques, who claimed it as his own, and that from him it was known as 'Jacques Ile.' Fearing that the women, instigated by the devil, were deceiving us, we visited the other island, with the holy determination to exterminate any enemies of your sacred Majesty thereon, but found the story of the women was true. The Frenchman Jacques had a hut near the water, where he lived with an Indian pagan as his wife. He had a liberal store of turtle's eggs, gathered in the sand, which we took from him, as also his carbine and forty pounds of ambergris, which he had collected from the sea, but did him no further harm. We took here another observation, finding the latitude 31 deg. 10 min. N."

The latitude mentioned by Drake indicates that he visited first what is now known as Cumberland Island, and later, Jekyl Island, the name by which the latter island is known being evidently a corruption of its early cognomen, the transition from Jacques Ile to Jekyl being easy and natural.

The next mention I find relative to Jekyl Island occurs in a volume published by Wm. Dampier, in 1729, entitled, "Two Voyages to the Bay of Campeachy." This eminent navigator, author and pirate, set out from Virginia in 1684, on a buccaneering expedition against the Spanish settlements. He says:

"The next morning, being now nearly arrived at the Florida coast, we landed upon an island in latitude 31 deg. 12 min. N. for a supply of fresh water."

The latitude indicates the location of Jekyl Island. Dampier continues:

"Near the spot where we landed we found an abundance of fresh water and also a few huts, which were inhabited by peaceable savages. Much surprised were we to find that they spoke a language in which were found occasionally French words. We soon learned that they were largely the descendants of a Frenchman who had long before lived upon the island and married many Indian wives. From him the place was called 'Jacques Island.' The natural depravity of the pagans appeared, as we noticed that the French words were few in their usual conversation, but that they had hoarded many French curses and bitter profanities, which they heaped upon us as we left the island, for no other reason, as we could conjecture, except that we had taken with us their cattle, weapons, furs, provisions and other articles which might be useful to us thereafter."

After this landing of Dampier, I find scanty mention of Jekyl Island prior to the founding of the Georgia colony under General Jas. E.

Oglethorpe, in 1733. The first settlement was at the present site of the city of Savannah, but later, General Oglethorpe determined upon Saint Simon's Island as the most advantageous location for a colony. There are three large islands off the Georgia coast: Cumberland, already mentioned as the landing place of Sir Francis Drake, is the most southerly; north of this is Jekyl Island, and still further north is the Island of Saint Simons. Both the other islands are plainly visible from Jekyl. To be near his settlement of a large colony on Saint Simon's Island, and still to have the isolation and dig-. nity proper to the gubernatorial state, Oglethorpe selected Jekyl as his own residence, and built there a commodious mansion of logs. Lady Oglethorpe, in one of her letters, speaks of having brought from the mainland and planted near the family mansion some roots of. yellow jessamine, not indigenous to the island, and the fact that a quantity of this jessamine is still growing near the solitary chimney already mentioned, although not found else-where upon the island, is confirmatory of the legend that this chimney marks the spot where stood the baronial log castle of the Oglethorpes.

General Oglethorpe was a soldier of tried and unquestioned valor, an educated and accomplished gentleman of great ability and pleasing address, to whose manly and martial figure scant justice is done in the otherwise admirable statue belonging to the Century Club of New York.

Prior to the founding of the Georgia colony the island appears to have been only occasionally visited by hunters or fishermen, and after this date the change of the original name, " Jacques Isle," to Jekyl, seems to have become generally recognized, the island being always spoken of as Jekyl in the correspondence ·and documents of Governor Oglethorpe.

After the founding of the Georgia colony, the records of the island are for some time reasonably complete. For the data to which I will have time to refer at present, I am almost entirely indebted to the courtesy of Colonel Jefferson Davis Twiggs, the Secretary

of the Georgia Historical Society, and a son
of the General Twiggs, whose gallantry and
bravery were conspicuous in the war with
Mexico. The collection of manuscripts and
public documents relative to the early settlement of the State is large, and fortunately
escaped the destruction which befell so many
similar collections during the civil war.

The Georgia colony was originally organized
as a home for unfortunate but industrious and
worthy people. The first prospectus stated
that, as colonists, all idle and vicious people
would be excluded, as also all married men dis-
posed to leave their families behind. Slavery
was forbidden. Among the people afterward
notable, connected with the early settlement,
were Charles and John Wesley and George
Whitefield. Charles Wesley was sent as secretary to General Oglethorpe and John as a mis-
sionary to the Indians. On the return of John
to England, in 1737, Whitefield was sent by the
trustees to take his place.

When General Oglethorpe established himself on Jekyl Island with his family, secretary

and servants, the island became virtually the
capital of the Georgia colony. Both General
and Lady Oglethorpe and the secretary often
visited Savannah, which, with the country
about it, continued to be the principal center
of population as long as Oglethorpe remained
in America, which was for a period of ten years.
This period, from 1733 to 1743, is the romantic
and picturesque period in the history of the
island, as the plan of General Oglethorpe to
make Saint Simon's Island the principal settlement, and Jekyl Island the government head-
quarters, was not carried out, and Jekyl Island,
after his return to England, seems to have
been substantially abandoned. Nearly all evi-
dences of the occupation of the island were
dissipated by time, and the island itself was
practically deserted for the greater part of a
century.

Among the manuscripts preserved in the
archives of the Georgia Historical Society are
various regulations prescribed by General Oglethorpe for the government of the colony, and
considerable correspondence passing between

LADY DOROTHY OGLETHORPE.

Reproduced from the miniature on ivory by Gainsborough,
now in the possession of Francis Bartlett, Esq., of Boston.

himself, his secretaries and Lady Oglethorpe, which are of interest as illustrating the experiences and hardships connected with the period of this first occupation of Jekyl Island.

In 1734 Lady Oglethorpe writes to her husband, then absent at Savannah. She says:

"Since your departure, my dearest husband, all the pigs have escaped into the dreadful wilderness about us, and we fear daily that they will be captured and eaten by the savages. The Chief, Altamaha, and his band, are still upon the island, and yesterday he came and begged tobacco and sugar, and also demanded of me our maid servant Elizabeth as his wife, much to her astonishment and terror. He was dressed in all his barbaric finery, painted and bedaubed in as many colors as the coat of Joseph, and decorated with feathers, bears' claws and bright colored shells, as befitted a man equipped for female conquest. The wretched pagan has already three wives, whom he treats worse than beasts of burden, and I think this somewhat influenced Elizabeth, as, had he been unmarried, the prospect of being

a queen, even of the wild and savage Tusca-
roras, might have moved her. These Indians
are soon to return northward, as the Choctaws
claim the country hereabout, and the Tusca-
roras, while boasting to fear nothing, yet love
their own scalps to remain where the good God
placed them.

During your absence I have again been
troubled by a slight but authentic attack of the
gout, and long unceasingly for your return."

In 1736, when Lady Oglethorpe was in Savannah, Charles Wesley writes her from Jekyl
Island thus:

"I have but this day returned from the trip
to the Ogeechee River, where I suffered many
hardships and privations from the inhospitable
weather. With my brother John, I preached
to the Indians, whenever we could find them in
any considerable numbers, although I fear but
little impression was made upon them. Their
simple and untutored minds find difficulty in
comprehending the beautiful doctrine of the
Trinity, or in realizing the sublimity of a pure
and sinless Saviour suffering untold agonies

for the crimes of wicked men. One of these pagans, whose mind had been heretofore in total darkness, when urged to become a Christian, retorted that Christians lied and cheated when buying furs and were drunkards, and said that, as these men were Christians, he would none of it, so hardened by the wiles of Satan are these unbelievers against the truths of the gospel.

"Last evening I wandered to the north end of the island and stood upon the narrow point, which your ladyship will recall as there projecting into the ocean. The vastness of the watery waste, as compared with my standing place, called to mind the briefness of human life, and the immensity of its consequences, and my surroundings inspired me to write a hymn, commencing:

Lo! on a narrow neck of land,
'Twixt two unbounded seas I stand,

which I trust may pleasure your ladyship, weak and feeble as it is when compared with the songs of the sweet psalmist of Israel. I feel that here, like Moses, I am a stranger in a strange land, and I pray hourly that when the night cometh, and when deep sleep falleth upon me, I may not be found without a wedding garment."

Extracts from a letter from John Wesley to General Oglethorpe illustrate some of the early experiences of this noted evangelist. He says:

"After leaving Jekyl Island came a most wearisome journey of five days through swamps and forests, when we reached the place for the annual council of the Choctaws, and found the savages gathered in great numbers. As I gazed upon the multitude of idolaters, to whom I would fain be the messenger bearing the good tidings of great joy, I was filled with a deep pity for their unhappy state, and, as a hen gathereth her chickens under her wings, felt to gladly labor until I enter the house appointed for all the living, to bring them within the fold purchased for a sin-laden world. I had with me as interpreter the half-breed, Mary Musgrove, and daily had meetings for instruction and prayer, and trust that the future may show that some of the seed thus sown has fallen upon good

ground. One woman was baptized. She was
of those which come out of great tribulation,
her husband and all her three children having
been drowned four days before in crossing the
Ogeechee River, and her happiness in the gospel caused me to feel that, like Job, the Master
had caused the widow's heart to sing for joy.
She was again married the day following her
baptism, and when I suggested longer days of
mourning, she only replied that her first husband was surely dead, and that his successor
was of much substance, having a cornfield and
a gun. I have acquired sundry words of the
language of the Choctaws, and long to be able
to speak to them in their mother tongue. I
doubt the interpreter, Mary Musgrove, who is
yet in the valley and shadow of darkness. To
speak to the idolatrous Choctaws in the Eng-
lish language is as the crackling of thorns under a
pot; is as one who would essay to draw out the
leviathan with a hook; who should seek to bind
the sweet influences of the Pleiades, or loose
the bands of Orion.

Verily the flesh is weak, for I cannot but

long for the day when again I may visit you
and enjoy the flesh-pots of Jekyl Island. I
can with difficulty eat the food of the savages.
Insects bite and destroy my sleep. I am as a
skeleton, and the evil one continually suggests
that I murmur at my lot, and seek an easier
way in which to serve the Lord."

In 1736 came to John Wesley the experience
of an earthly love, but the woman who was its
object married another, and this disappoint-
ment caused the great evangelist to free his
mind as to the woman and her husband in such
language that he was indicted for libel, and
fled to England to escape imprisonment, whereupon George Whitefield was chosen by the
trustees as his successor, and arrived at Jekyl
Island in 1737.

In further illustration of early life upon the
island, I copy one of the letters of Lady Oglethorpe to Sir Theophilus, the father of her husband.

"DEAR AND HONORED PARENT:

I take my pen in hand to inform you that
my dear husband and myself are well and I

hope these few lines may find you in the enjoy-
ment of the same great blessing. We are now
established in our new home on Jekyl Island,
and I would fain give you a picture of this
abode of the Governor of this promising colony.
The mansion is built of pine logs, plastered,
where plastered at all, with clay, and sur-
rounded by a dense forest. The house is very
large and commodious, but lacking many of the
conveniences of our pleasant home in Surrey.
We sleep on beds made of pine leaves, which
are most comfortable and exhale a balsamic
fragrance supposed to be conducive to health.
Our floors are of split pine logs, and about the
walls are wooden pegs upon which to hang our
gowns. Much of our china was broken on our
journey hither, and we use instead the pewter
mugs and plates brought for our servants. A
few red savages are near us, living in wigwams,
who beg often for tobacco, but bring us in return an abundance of venison and fish. The
secretary of the colony, Charles Wesley, dwells
with us upon the island, and is zealous to save
the souls of the Indians who come hither to

hunt and to fish. He baptized a week since
one Indian and made him a part of Christian-
ity, but later, for what reasons we cannot divine,
though certainly through evil temptations of
the father of idolatry, the devil, he suddenly
cast off the Christian religion and abandoned
the true, divine worship. Mr. Wesley has also
the gift of verse, and has written many sweet
hymns, which we sing in our family worship.
Last week came several cloudy and dismal
days, which he reported to us had inspired him
to write a hymn contrasting the shadowed life
here with the brightness of that which is to
come. It begins thus :

> No need of the sun in that day
>> Which never is followed by night,
> Where Jesus's beauties display
>> A pure and a permanent light.

A few days later he wrote another, after a
most brilliant sunset, which we had all sur-
veyed with delight :

> With glorious clouds encompassed round,
>> Whom angels dimly see,
> Will the unsearchable be found,
>> Or God appear to me.

From these lines you will see his readiness to draw instructive lessons from all the incidents of daily life, although, as you will see later, sometimes his hymns come near to involve him in trouble.

He is of much self-denial and oftentimes of almost ascetic life, as appears from one of his hymns commencing,

I do suspect some danger nigh
When I do feel delight.

From what I have written, you must not infer that we live altogether a lonely and quiet life. We have twice visited Charleston, the principal city of South Carolina, where we have been sumptuously entertained by the governor and principal citizens, whom we have, of course, invited to visit us in return. Recently we received word that our invitations would be accepted. We had informed them of our primitive mode of life, which they fully realized, having been in similar conditions themselves. Last Wednesday we were startled by a long blast from a conch shell, and on going to the beach saw a large party approaching in a flat

boat, men, women, negroes, horses and dogs.
They were soon disembarked and at the house,
where General Oglethorpe made them welcome
with an abundance of rum made by the Puri-
tans in that part of America called New Eng.
land. They then told us that not to overtax our
hospitalities, they had brought with them an
abundance of food and servants, and proposed
to go at once to some suitable place upon the
shore and roast oysters. We set out for a cove
about a mile distant from our home. The
progress towards it was a striking and curious
pageant. First, marched as trumpeter, a stal-
wart negro, blowing a conch shell and produc-
ng a dismal and incessant blare. Then General Oglethorpe on horseback, with myself behind him on a pillion, and a negro on a mule,
carrying my best hat in a box, lest it be destroyed by the trees and bushes. Then our
family coach, with one wheel missing from an
encounter with a stump, the axle being held up
by a pole, and within the family of Governor
Pickens, his wife, sister and a niece, Miss Mercy
Pickens. Then two open wagons with the

other ladies of the party, and some jugs of rum
and boxes of food. About these rode the
gentlemen on horses and mules, among them
Mr. George Moultrie, a gallant young man who
is soon to wed Miss Mercy before named.
Around the cavalcade swarmed the negroes,
shouting and laughing, rolling their white eyes,
and showing their white teeth in contrast to
their shining black skins, and singing songs full
of melody and pathos. They seemed to bear
the names of all the heathen divinities and
historic heroes. I recall Diana, Flora, Phyllis,
Cæsar, Pompey, Hannibal, Jupiter, and many
more.

The road to the beach, while rude and rough
for vehicles by reason of roots and stumps,
is of wonderful beauty, bordered with great
growths of evergreen oaks and magnolias, with
thickets of myrtle and bay, and a carpet of
dwarf palmetto, all of most lustrous green, and
the trees often festooned or bound together
with trailing garlands of pale, gray moss. The
most perfect art could devise nothing more
beautiful than the tropical glories of this forest

drive. When we reached the cove the negroes waded into the water and brought ashore great baskets of oysters, which they roasted in a fire kindled from branches of the fragrant pine. General Oglethorpe brewed a large tub of rum punch, while I made a bowl of delicious sanga- ree with wine from your own cellar, which has been with us from the time of our leaving dear old England. No one neglected these bever- ages, and with the oysters, the cheese and other viands with which we were provided, a royal banquet was enjoyed. Many of the gentlemen were nearly overcome with the rum punch, although insisting that it was the roasted oys- ters which made their legs unsteady, and this had nearly led Mr. Wesley into serious trouble with Mr. Moultrie, whose almost maudlin at- tentions to his sweetheart, Miss Mercy, were constant and even annoying to her.

As Mr. Wesley drank no punch, they insisted he should sing, and he commenced one of his hymns which is a favorite with us :

> "Depth of mercy, can there be
> Mercy still reserved for me ? "——

" Hold," shouted Mr. Moultrie, "none of your
damned presumption. Mercy is not reserved
for you or any of your kind. She is mine and
mine alone." General Oglethorpe interfered
and endeavored to explain, but Mr. Moultrie
would listen to nothing, and proposed to give
the Secretary a drubbing on the spot. I suc-
ceeded in quieting him, and asked Mr. Wesley
to substitute another hymn, whereupon he commenced :

"The day of jubilee is come,
    Return ye ransomed sinners home."

"What!" shouted my husband, "are you
ordering away my guests on their very arrival?
None of your foolishness." "Sir," said Mr.
Wesley, " I was not addressing your guests. I
do not consider them as ransomed sinners."

" What do you mean?" said Governor Pickens; "go and drum your nonsense into the
woolly head of the negroes."

The riot was presently at an end, Mr. Wesley
returning to the house, and was forgotten after
the gentlemen had slept off their potations.

The party remained with us for three days,

and until the rum was exhausted, the gentlemen hunting daily and the ladies riding about
the island and telling us all the gossip and
scandals of Charleston.   The hunters brought
in an abundance of game, and this was cooked
and served by the negro servants brought with
our visitors, whose skill made us almost regret
General Oglethorpe's determination that no
slaves shall be held in the Georgia colony.

No more at present from your dutiful
daughter,

DOROTHY OGLETHORPE."

I will conclude with extracts from two letters
of George Whitefield to General Oglethorpe,
written with an interval of about thirty years
between, which illustrate a curious phase in
the life of this famous preacher.   Whitefield,
soon after his arrival in Georgia, built what he
called an Orphanage, an institution where poor
and neglected children could be cared for,
educated and fitted for useful lives.   During
his subsequent years this institution was his
constant care; he solicited money for it in all
his fields of labor.   In 1739 he writes to Gen-

eral Oglethorpe thus, he being at that time in
Savannah :

"I have just this day reached Jekyl Island,
after an absence of three weeks, the most of
which time was spent at the Orphanage and in
its vicinity. The dear children are well and
happy. Last February I decided to plant a
farm, with the view of using the gain there-
from to carry forward the work of the Orphanage. I am more than ever convinced of the
wisdom of excluding slavery from the Georgia
colony. Slavery is the sum of all villainies
and abominations, and could I secure money
in other ways, I would never touch again the
contributions from the Carolinas and Virginia,
made by the slave owners, whose wealth is
gained from the unpaid labor of wretched
negroes or by the infamous traffic in human
flesh. Scarcely shall such men inherit eternal
life. The gates of the celestial city shall rarely
open to those who traffic in the bodies and
souls of men. They have made a covenant
with death and with hell they are at agreement.

I hired several people who had no homes or

employment to cultivate the plantation, and now that the crops are gathered, I am in despair to find that there is no gain, but a loss. The Master hath said, the laborer is worthy of his hire, but the wages of the workman absorb the value of the harvest and more. I entered upon the work with lofty hopes, but pride goeth before destruction and a haughty spirit before a fall. Let not him that girdeth on his harness boast himself as he that putteth it off."

Nearly thirty years after the writing of this letter, and near the close of Whitefield's life, I find another letter from him to General Oglethorpe. The General had long before returned to England. Whitefield had spent the intervening years in public work, having seven times crossed the Atlantic, preaching with wonderful effect in all parts of the New World, but having always in mind his Orphanage, for which he constantly labored and solicited aid. The letter runs thus:

"MY DEAR AND HONORED FRIEND

I am but now returned from a trip through Virginia and the Carolinas, during which I

REV. GEORGE WHITEFIELD.

From the portrait by William Hogarth, owned by the
Century Club of New York.

made a short visit to the Orphanage, which is as ever dear to my heart. The recollection of your encouragement and help in this valiant work; of the pleasant years when I was often with you at Jekyl Island, cheered by your wise and helpful counsel, have minded me to again write you something of myself and my labors. I am come to the time in life when the grasshopper is a burden; my strength is weakness, my days are swifter than a weaver's shuttle. As William Shakespeare—a man given overmuch to vain imaginings, yet whose lips ofttimes are touched with celestial fire, as he has said:

Like as the waves make toward the pebbled shore,
So do our minutes hasten to their end.

I trust that my labors in the Master's work have not been in vain, yet, as I consider my days and their approaching end, chiefly do I value myself upon the many children whom the dear Orphanage has transformed from impending lives of vice and sin to faithful servants of the Master. Three years since a Carolinian,

who at one of our meetings had found the pearl
of great price, gave me three healthy negroes,
told me of the great gain in the cultivation of
tobacco, and that a tobacco plantation would of
itself nearly maintain the Orphanage. I took
the money which had been contributed for the
good work, bought a small plantation in South
Carolina, as slavery was forbidden in Georgia,
bought also nine other strong negro men and
women, and planted tobacco. My agent has
each year secured bountiful crops. The Lord
has abundantly blessed our labors. The negroes work from sunrise to sunset in the fields,
and by moonlight cultivate the maize, which is
their food. The clothing for all costs scarcely
a pound in the year, and having to pay them
no wages nor to buy them food, the results are
most hopeful. Daily and nightly do I praise
the Lord for these bountiful harvests, and pray
that He whose mercy endureth forever may
continue to bless our fields, and to cause the
labor of these negro slaves to bear abundant
fruit in the salvation of the many little ones

who are ready to perish. Verily the word
fitly spoken by my adviser of the tobacco
plantation has been as apples of gold in pict-
ures of silver.

But, my friend, long and dearly loved, I
must come to an end. Perchance no more
shall I gaze into thy eyes and grasp thy hand
upon this earth; with me the fashion of this
world passeth away, but the love which is
stronger than death is my stay and my comfort
forever."

It has been with me a labor of love to rescue
from undeserved oblivion some few of the incidents in what may be termed the halcyon days
of Jekyl Island. During my stay at the Club
House, and since, in conversation with the
members, I have found no one who had searched
out, or was in any way familiar with, the period
of its occupation by Oglethorpe. Even the
vague tradition that it had been thus occupied
was often questioned. But even the meagre
glimpse which I have been able to afford of
these picturesque ten years gives to the spot a
much needed historic interest. Instead of be-

ing, as generally believed, an island, dull and
uninviting, where a few negroes had cultivated
and then abandoned small cotton fields, and
where a pleasant winter climate was its sole
excuse for being, it is seen to be linked with
events romantic and far reaching in our national
life. We may in imagination picture General
Oglethorpe and his lovely wife entertaining
with royal hospitality the thirsty governors of
North Carolina and South Carolina, with their
escort of fair women and brave men. Through
the majestic groves of pine, oak and magnolia,
and across the broad savannas, we may see
the brilliant array of huntsmen gaily capari-
soned, following their hounds, while the cheer-
ing bugle blasts echo far and away through the
forest. We see the huntsmen returning home
with brush and game, welcomed by the courtly
dames as became a gallant and victorious
band of warriors; and as the sun goes down
we may see the powdered heroes leading
through the mazes of the stately minuet, on the
floor of logs, the ladies, brave in ruff, brocade
and farthingale.

Under the fragrant pines we may see the council of war, as General Oglethorpe with his subordinates plans the brilliant though unsuccessful campaign against the Spanish city of St. Augustine. Here, too, we see the youthful Wesley, the founder of Methodism, scarcely yet conscious of his mission and destiny as he wanders dreamily along the shores of the sounding sea, brooding the problems of profoundest moment, or shaping the sacred hymns, which have since, in all climes and tongues, been the consolation of humanity. And here, too, we see George Whitefield, the most entrancing pulpit orator of the last two centuries, seeking often, after his conflict with the hosts of sin, rest for body and mind in the forests of Jekyl Island; and, among the same wide-spreading evergreen oaks, gray with their trailing garlands of moss, under which we may wander to-day, nursing for the life-long battle his fascinating and magical eloquence. Surely, Prospero, waving anew his magic wand, could never summon from the vasty deep an island more historically picturesque.

www.ingramcontent.com/pod-product-compliance
Lightning Source LLC
Chambersburg PA
CBHW031816090426

42739CB00008B/1301